FACTS ABOUT
NUNAVUT

Nunavut is in Northern Canada.

ARCTIC
OCEAN

GREENLAND

BAFFIN
BAY

NUNAVUT

UKON   NORTHWEST TERRITORIES

BRITISH
COLUMBIA   ALBERTA   SASK.   MANITOBA

HUDSON
BAY

QUEBEC

ONTARIO

Iqaluit is the largest community in Nunavut.

It gets very cold
in Nunavut.

We can see northern lights in Nunavut.

There are lots of animals
in Nunavut.

There are inuksuit
(inukshuks) in Nunavut.